NEW MATHS FRAMEWORKING

Matches the revised KS3 Framework

Helen and Simon Greaves

Contents

Exercise 1A **The calendar**

This exercise will give you practice in

○ using a calendar to solve time problems

Here are two pages from the calendar for 2008. Use these pages to answer the questions.

June 2008						
Su	Mo	Tu	We	Th	Fr	Sa
1	2	3	4	5	6	7
8	9	10	11	12	13	14
15	16	17	18	19	20	21
22	23	24	25	26	27	28
29	30					

July 2008						
Su	Mo	Tu	We	Th	Fr	Sa
		1	2	3	4	5
6	7	8	9	10	11	12
13	14	15	16	17	18	19
20	21	22	23	24	25	26
27	28	29	30	31		

1 How many days does the month of July have? _____

2 How many Tuesdays are there in June? _____

3 How many Sundays are there in July? _____

4 On which day of the week does July 2008 start? _____

5 On what date is the third Monday in July? _____

6 On which days are the following dates? _____

   a 22nd July _____

   b 4th June _____

   c 29th June _____

   d 19th July _____

7 Sam goes on holiday on the 7th June 2008. He is away one week. On which date does he return? _____

8 Bethany goes on holiday on the 25th June and is away for a fortnight. On what date does she return? _____

9 Kyla goes on holiday on 21st June and returns on 2nd July. How many full days was she o: holiday for? _____

Exercise 1B   Time

This exercise will give you practice in
- converting between 12- and 24-hour clock times

1 Write the 24-hour times for each of the following. The first one has been done for you.

    a 3.00 pm *15:00* _____   **b** 9.45 pm _____

    c 10.35 pm _____   **d** 9.30 am _____

    e 11.52 pm _____   **f** 2.56 pm _____

2 Write the 12-hour times for each of the following.

    a 19:00 _____

    b 14:54 _____

    c 16:45 _____

    d 15:25 _____

    e 09:45 _____

    f 13:56 _____

3 Complete the chart.

Time	12-hour clock	24-hour clock
Half past 6 in the morning	6.30 am	06:30
		14:00
	8.30 pm	
10 o' clock in the evening		
		07:15
	2.00 am	
		23:30
Half past midnight		
	3.45 pm	
		02:50

Exercise 2A Number sequences

This exercise will give you practice in

- recognising and extending number sequences

1 **a** Add 10 each time to get to the top of the stairs.

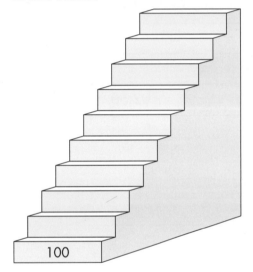

b Add 20 each time to get to the top of the stairs.

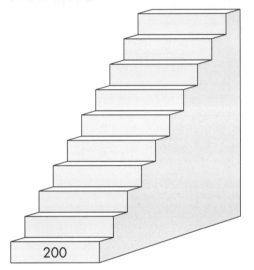

c Add 25 each time to get to the top of the stairs.

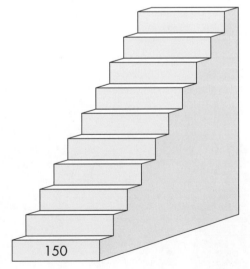

d Subtract 10 each time to get to the bottom of the stairs.

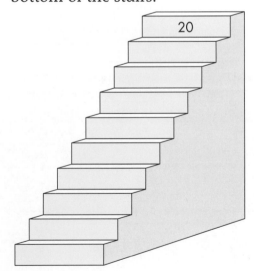

e Subtract 20 each time to get to the bottom of the stairs.

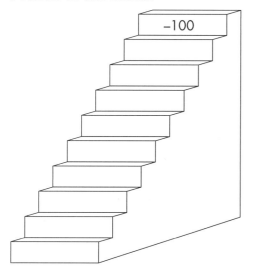

−100

f Subtract 25 each time to get to the bottom of the stairs.

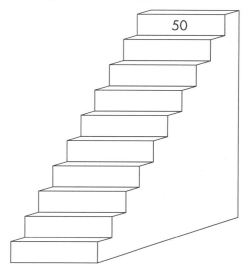

50

2 **a** Write down all the multiples of 6 in order from −60 to 60.

b Write down all the multiples of 8 in order from −80 to 80.

c Which multiples appear in both lists **a** and **b**?

3 Using your two lists of multiples from **Question 2**, complete the table below.

Start	Add/subtract	Finish
8	+ one lot of 8	
16	+ three lots of 8	
12	+ two lots of 6	
−6	− three lots of 6	
−24	+ four lots of 8	
−64	+ three lots of 8	
56	− four lots of 8	
36	− six lots of 6	

Exercise 2B Odd and even numbers

This exercise will give you practice in

- recognising odd and even numbers and their properties

1 Complete each addition in the following tables.

	Even				
	+	4	6	2	8
Even	6	10			
	2				
	8				
	4				
	10				

	Odd				
	+	7	11	3	13
Odd	1				
	5				
	9				
	3				
	7				

	Odd				
	+	7	3	9	11
Even	6				
	2				
	8				
	4				
	10				

2 Here are some digit cards.

| 3 | 4 | 7 | 8 |

Use all four digit cards to make:

a   the largest even number   _____

b   the smallest odd number   _____

c   the largest odd number   _____

d   the smallest even number   _____

Use three of the digit cards to make:

e   an even number that is less than 1000   _____

f   an odd number that is less than 500   _____

Exercise 2C   Rounding

This exercise will give you practice in
- rounding any positive integer less than 1000 to the nearest 10 or 100
- rounding some four-digit numbers to the nearest 1000

1 Round each of these numbers to the nearest multiple of 10.

a   64 _____   **b**   72 _____   **c**   89 _____

d   23 _____   **e**   65 _____   **f**   14 _____

g   26 _____   **h**   31 _____   **i**   25 _____

j   77 _____   **k**   66 _____   **l**   34 _____

2 Round each of these numbers to the nearest multiple of 100.

a   734 _____   **b**   576 _____   **c**   212 _____

d   788 _____   **e**   899 _____   **f**   150 _____

g   129 _____   **h**   233 _____   **i**   643 _____

j   349 _____   **k**   743 _____   **l**   379 _____

3 Round each of these numbers to the nearest thousand.

a	3400	**b**	1200	**c**	7800	**d**	8900
e	6100	**f**	6500	**g**	9200	**h**	5500
i	6800	**j**	3200	**k**	4500	**l**	1300

4 Round the numbers in the table to the nearest multiple of 10 and 100. The first one has been done for you.

Number	Nearest multiple of 10	Nearest multiple of 100
341	*340*	*300*
136		
765		
551		
899		
224		
665		

Exercise 2D Square numbers

This exercise will give you practice in

- using and learning squares of numbers to at least 12 × 12

1 Write a multiplication fact and a square number fact for each picture using the example below as a guide.

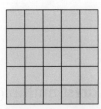

5 × 5 = 25
5² = 25

a

_____

_____

b

_____

_____

c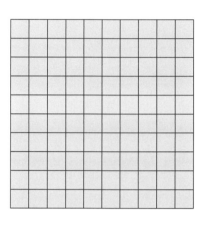

_____

_____

d

_____

_____

f

e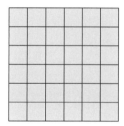

_____

_____

g

_____

_____

2) Complete each of the following.

a ____^{2} = 36   **b** 10 × 10 = ____   **c** ____^{2} = 81   **d** 8 × ____ = 64

e ____^{2} = 16   **f** ____ × ____ = 49   **g** 6 × 6 = ____   **h** ____^{2} = 4

i 7^2 = ____   **j** ____ × ____ = 1   **k** ____^{2} = 100   **l** 9 × 9 = ____

m ____^{2} = 25   **n** 11 × 11 = ____   **o** 12^2 = ____   **p** ____^{2} = 121

Exercise 2E Sequences

This exercise will give you practice in

- generating and describing simple integer sequences

1 Write the next 10 numbers in each of these number sequences using the rule shown.

a The rule is add on 2 each time.

22, 24, 26, ☐ , ☐ , ☐ , ☐ , ☐ , ☐ , ☐ , ☐ , ☐ , ☐

b The rule is add on 3 each time.

36, 39, 42, ☐ , ☐ , ☐ , ☐ , ☐ , ☐ , ☐ , ☐ , ☐ , ☐

c The rule is add on 4 each time.

12, 16, 20, ☐ , ☐ , ☐ , ☐ , ☐ , ☐ , ☐ , ☐ , ☐ , ☐

d The rule is subtract 3 each time.

72, 69, 66, ☐ , ☐ , ☐ , ☐ , ☐ , ☐ , ☐ , ☐ , ☐ , ☐

e The rule is subtract 10 each time.

320, 310, 300, ☐ , ☐ , ☐ , ☐ , ☐ , ☐ , ☐ , ☐ , ☐ , ☐

f The rule is subtract 5 each time.

70, 65, 60, ☐ , ☐ , ☐ , ☐ , ☐ , ☐ , ☐ , ☐ , ☐ , ☐

2 Write the next 5 numbers in each of these number sequences and then write the rule.

a 3, 8, 13, ☐ , ☐ , ☐ , ☐ , ☐

The rule is _____

b 31, 28, 25, ☐ , ☐ , ☐ , ☐ , ☐

The rule is _____

c 98, 92, 86, ☐ , ☐ , ☐ , ☐ , ☐

The rule is _____

d 55, 66, 77, ☐ , ☐ , ☐ , ☐ , ☐

The rule is _____

Exercise 3A **Currency**

This exercise will give you practice in

- solving real-life problems using coins

1 An apple costs 21p. Write down three different ways you could pay for the apple using coins.

2 A bottle of water costs 46p. Write down three different ways you could pay for the bottle of water using coins.

3 What is the fewest number of coins that could be used to make the following amounts?

a 9p

b 16p

c 33p

d 68p

4 Here are some items for sale in a snack bar.

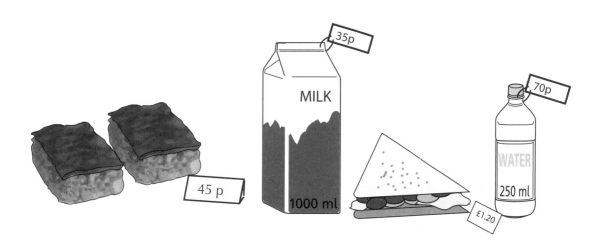

a **i** How much will it cost to buy a flapjack and a carton of milk?

ii What is the fewest number of coins you would need to pay for them? List them.

b **i** How much will it cost to buy a sandwich and a bottle of water?

ii What is the fewest number of coins you would need to pay for them? List them.

c **i** How much will it cost to buy a flapjack and a bottle of water?

ii What is the fewest number of coins you would need to pay for them? List them.

d **i** How much will it cost to buy a carton of milk and a sandwich?

ii How much change would there be if you paid for them with a £2 coin?

iii What is the fewest number of coins you could have in your change? List them.

Exercise 3B Words and numbers

This exercise will give you practice in
- reading and writing numbers in figures and words

1 Write these numbers in figures.

a twenty-seven _____

b thirty-four _____

c one hundred and fifty-two _____

d three hundred and sixty-four _____

27

twenty-seven

e   seven hundred and forty-one _____

f   one thousand one hundred and one _____

g   two thousand four hundred and forty _____

h   nine thousand five hundred and twenty-one _____

2 Write these numbers in words.

a   35 _____

b   56 _____

c   179 _____

d   284 _____

e   997 _____

f   1678 _____
     _____

g   1002 _____
     _____

h   1999 _____
     _____

3 Kamal is a second-hand car salesman. He wants to put the price of each car on
its windscreen in numbers. Write in the price of each car on its windscreen.

a   two thousand five hundred pounds   b   one thousand one hundred and
                                                    ninety-nine pounds

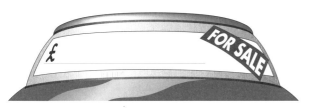   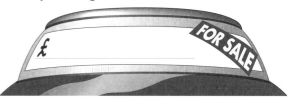

c   nine hundred and ninety-nine pounds   d   five hundred pounds

e two thousand and ninety-nine pounds

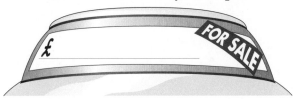

4 Which is the cheapest car in **Question 3**? _____

Exercise 3C Addition

This exercise will give you practice in
- adding together two whole numbers

1 Use any method to work out each of the following additions.

a 34 + 57	**b** 72 + 78	**c** 66 + 23
d 92 + 34	**e** 46 + 59	**f** 91 + 23
g 32 + 77	**h** 65 + 56	**i** 94 + 67

2 Use any method to work out each of the following additions.

a 174 + 75	**b** 362 + 62	**c** 473 + 66
d 286 + 345	**e** 765 + 434	**f** 676 + 545

g   975 + 323   h   778 + 334   i   265 + 799

3 Choose one number from Box A and one number from Box B to make five addition calculations. Work out the answer to each of your calculations in the box below.

Box A			
165	757	334	28
742	654	224	

Box B			
72	659	99	286
462	889	999	

Exercise 3D **Subtraction**

This exercise will give you practice in
- subtracting two whole numbers

1 Use any method to work out each of the following subtractions.

a   74 − 34   b   78 − 72   c   66 − 23

d   92 − 34   e   46 − 39   f   91 − 23

g 98 – 77   **h** 65 – 56   **i** 94 – 67

2 Use any method to work out each of the following subtractions.

a 286 – 145   **b** 765 – 434   **c** 778 – 334

d 174 – 77   **e** 362 – 64   **f** 634 – 545

g 975 – 386   **h** 473 – 66   **i** 265 – 199

3 Choose one number from Box A and one number from Box B to make five subtraction calculations. Work out the answer to each of your calculations in the box below.

Remember, your first number needs to be bigger than your second number.

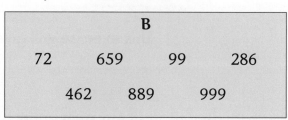

A			
165	757	334	28
742	654	224	

B			
72	659	99	286
462	889	999	

Exercise 3E   **Using a calculator**

This exercise will give you practice in

- using a calculator for addition, subtraction, multiplication and division

1 Use a calculator to work out these calculations. Write your answers in the spaces provided. Remember to enter the numbers carefully and check the operation!

a   4823 + 767 _____

b   6752 + 3467 _____

c   3923 + 567 _____

d   7465 + 986 _____

e   2232 + 4466 _____

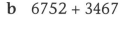

f   7654 – 3345 _____

g   8345 – 641 _____

h   4588 – 323 _____

i   8822 – 222 _____

j   4294 – 4291 _____

k   72 × 44 _____

l   78 × 22 _____

m   99 × 100 _____

n   156 × 223 _____

o   5724 ÷ 36 _____

p   14 736 ÷ 48 _____

q   79 856 ÷ 1426 _____

r   91 416 ÷ 52 _____

2 a   2   3   5   4

Use any of the numbers and the + key on your calculator to make 10.
Write down your calculation.

_____

b   2   6   7   4

Use any of the numbers and the + key on your calculator to make 17.
Write down your calculation.

_____

c   5   2   4   8

Use any of the numbers and the + key on your calculator to make 14.
Write down your calculation.

_____

d   7   4   9   8   1   2

Use any of the numbers and the `+` key on your calculator to make 20.
Write down your calculation.

_____

e   14   11   5   8   3

Use any of the numbers and the `-` key on your calculator to make 1.
Write down your calculation.

_____

f   17   3   7   4   2

Use any of the numbers and the `-` key on your calculator to make 6.
Write down your calculation.

_____

Exercise 3F   **Negative numbers**

This exercise will give you practice in

- ordering a set of positive and negative integers
- calculating a temperature rise and fall across 0°C

1   Put each set of numbers in order from smallest to largest.

a   2, 7, –2, 3, 5, –3, 0   _____

b   –7, 4, –5, 6, 1, –1, 2   _____

c   9, 6, –5, 4, –3, –4, 2, 7, –2, 0   _____

d   6, 4, –2, –3, 9, 7, –4, 6, 0, –1   _____

2   Look at the thermometers and answer the questions.

a
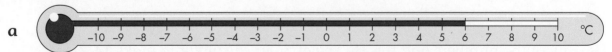

If the temperature increases by 3°C what will the temperature be?   _____

b

If the temperature falls by 5°C what will the temperature be?   _____

c

If the temperature falls by 4°C what will the temperature be? _____

d

If the temperature increases by 6°C what will the temperature be? _____

e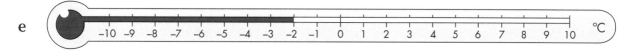

If the temperature increases by 2°C what will the temperature be? _____

f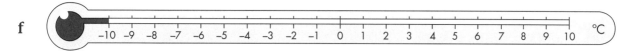

If the temperature increases by 15°C what will the temperature be? _____

g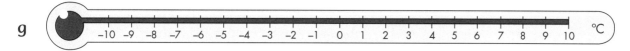

If the temperature decreases by 20°C what will the temperature be? _____

h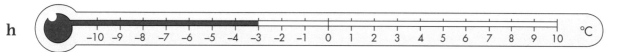

If the temperature increases by 12°C what will the temperature be? _____

Exercise 3G Multiplying by 10 and 100

This exercise will give you practice in
- multiplying positive integers by 10 or 100
- recognising the place value of numbers

Number bingo

Play this game with the person next to you.

a   Take it in turns to choose one of the operations and one of the numbers from the line below.

| ×10 | ×100 | | 500 | 45 | 95 | 30 | 40 | 350 | 16 | 60 | 7 | 10 | 12 | 8 | 200 | 9 |

b Multiply them to make one of the numbers in the grid below.

c If you were right, cross the number out on the grid.

d The winner is the person that crosses out five numbers in a line in any direction.

1600	450	400	100	120
3500	900	2000	70	1600
300	600	1200	700	3500
5000	3000	80	800	950
90	6000	4500	9500	160

2 Complete the multiplication grids.

a

×	10	100
55		
650		
31		
433		

b

×	10	100
6		
24		
72		
67		

c

×	10	100
333		
47		
82		
77		

3 Look at these numbers. In each number one digit is red. Write down what this digit represents.

a 45 395 _____

b 23 307 _____

c 65 788 _____

d 50 211 _____

e 96 473 _____

f 57 699 _____

g 52 147 _____

h 52 361 _____

Exercise 4A Length and perimeter

This exercise will give you practice in
- drawing straight lines accurately
- converting measurements between millimetres and centimetres and vice versa
- calculating the perimeter of a rectangle by adding the lengths of its sides
- calculating the perimeter of a rectangle using the formula **perimeter = 2 lengths + 2 widths**

1 Draw accurately in the space below lines of the following lengths. Label your lines.

   a   3 cm   **b**   4 cm   **c**   20 mm   **d**   40 mm

2 Convert the following measurements into centimetres.

   a   45 mm   **b**   30 mm   **c**   27 mm   **d**   68 mm

3 Convert the following measurements into millimetres.

   a   6 cm   **b**   12 cm   **c**   3 cm   **d**   4.5 cm

4 Calculate the perimeter of each of the following rectangles.

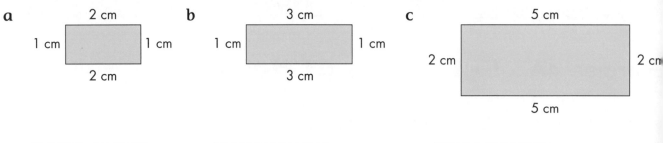

a   2 cm

1 cm   1 cm

2 cm

b   3 cm

1 cm   1 cm

3 cm

c   5 cm

2 cm   2 cm

5 cm

_____   _____   _____

_____   _____   _____

5 Calculate the perimeter of the following rectangles using the formula
perimeter = 2 lengths + 2 widths. Show your working.

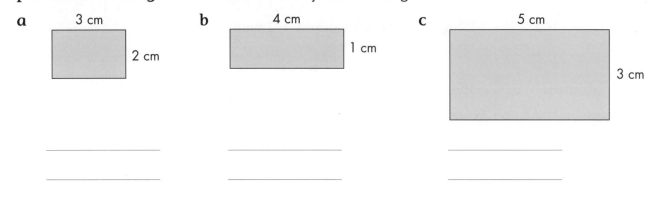

a   3 cm

2 cm

b   4 cm

1 cm

c   5 cm

3 cm

_____   _____   _____

_____   _____   _____

_____   _____   _____

6 Carole wants to put a fence around her vegetable
garden. She draws a sketch of the garden to help her.

How much fencing will she need? Show your working.

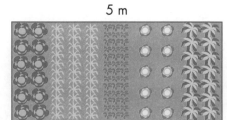

5 m

2 m

_____

_____

_____

Exercise 4B   Area

This exercise will give you practice in

- ● calculating the area of rectangles and other simple shapes
  using a counting method
- ● calculating the area of a rectangle or square using the formula
  area = length × breadth

1 **a** Find the area of the rectangle in cm^2 if the rectangle is made of up squares that measure 1 cm × 1 cm.

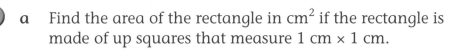

_____

b Find the area of the patio in m^2 if all of the patio slabs measure 1 m × 1 m.

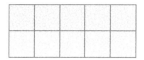

_____

2 David and Alisha are buying new tiles for their kitchen floor. How many 1 m^2 floor tiles will they need to cover the floor?

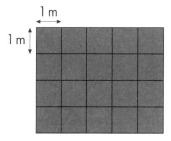

_____

_____

3 Find the area of each of the following shapes using the formula **area = length × breadth**. Show your working.

a 2 cm
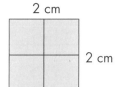
2 cm

b 3 m
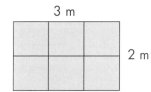
2 m

c 4 cm
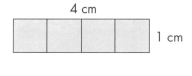
1 cm

_____   _____   _____

d 5 m

1 m

e 4 m
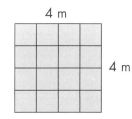
4 m

f 8 cm
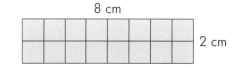
2 cm

_____   _____   _____

4 Which of the shapes in **Question 3** have the same area?

_____

Exercise 4C 3-D shapes and nets

This exercise will give you practice in
- learning the names of some regular 3-D shapes
- recognising which type of net makes an open cube
- recognising how many faces, vertices and edges that regular 3-D shapes have

1 Fill in the blanks to name the following regular 3-D shapes:

a   **b** 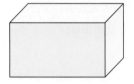   **c** 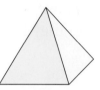   **d**

c__b__   c__b__i__   square-based py__a__i__   t__t__a__ed__

2 Circle the net you think will make an open cube. The base has been shaded to help you.

a   **b** 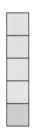   **c**   **d**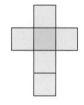

3 A cuboid has six faces, eight vertices and twelve edges.

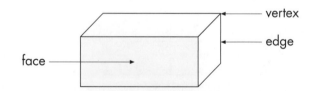

How many faces, vertices and edges do each of these 3-D shapes have?

a   **b** 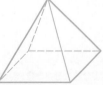   **c**

Faces _____   Faces _____   Faces _____

Vertices _____   Vertices _____   Vertices _____

Edges _____   Edges _____   Edges _____

Exercise 4D   Perimeters of regular polygons

This exercise will give you practice in

- calculating the perimeter of a regular polygon by measuring its sides
- calculating the perimeter of a regular polygon by using the formula

   perimeter = length of side × number of sides

1 Calculate the perimeter of each of the following regular polygons by using a ruler to measure each side.

a    b 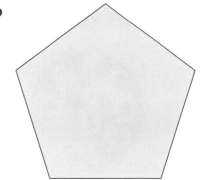   c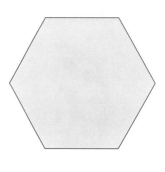

_____   _____   _____

2 Work out the perimeter of each of these regular polygons using the formula **perimeter = length of side × number of sides**.

a
2 cm

b
5 cm

c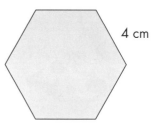
4 cm

_____   _____   _____

_____   _____   _____

3 a   Calculate the perimeter of the regular pentagon shown.

2 cm

_____

  b   What would the perimeter be if each side were:

   i   3 cm _____

   ii 4 cm _____

   iii 6 cm _____

Exercise 5A   Improper fractions and mixed numbers

This exercise will give you practice in
- using fractions
- converting improper fractions into mixed numbers

1 What fraction of pizza is left? Write each fraction in numbers and words.

a

_____

_____

b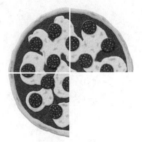

_____

_____

c

_____

_____

d

_____

_____

e

_____

_____

f

_____

_____

g

_____

_____

h

_____

_____

i

_____

_____

2 Look at the cakes. Describe the pieces left in two ways, as a mixed number and as an improper fraction. The first one has been done for you.

a

$$1\frac{3}{4} \qquad \frac{7}{4}$$

b

c

d

e

f

g

Exercise 5B Equivalent fractions

This exercise will give you practice in

- recognising and finding equivalent fractions

1 Colour in the amounts that make a half.

a   b   c   d   e

  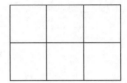  

2 Colour in the amounts that make a quarter.

a   b   c

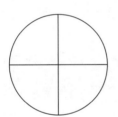 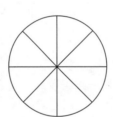 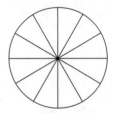

3 Find the equivalent fractions. One has been done for you.

$$\frac{1}{2} = \frac{4}{8}$$

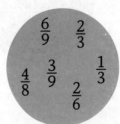

$\frac{1}{2}$ $\frac{2}{4}$ $\frac{3}{4}$ $\frac{6}{8}$ $\frac{9}{12}$ $\frac{5}{10}$

$\frac{6}{9}$ $\frac{2}{3}$ $\frac{4}{8}$ $\frac{3}{9}$ $\frac{1}{3}$ $\frac{2}{6}$

_____

_____

_____

_____

4 Colour in the equivalent fractions for a third.

      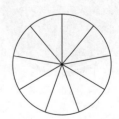

5 Colour in the equivalent fractions for a fifth.

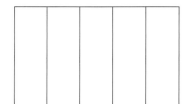 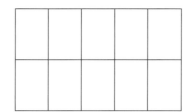 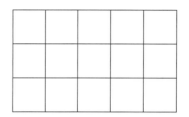

Exercise 5C Making equivalent fractions

This exercise will give you practice in

- finding equivalent fractions

1 Fill in the missing number in each of these equivalent fractions.

a $\dfrac{1}{2} = \dfrac{}{4}$
b $\dfrac{1}{4} = \dfrac{}{8}$
c $\dfrac{2}{3} = \dfrac{}{6}$
d $\dfrac{3}{4} = \dfrac{}{8}$
e $\dfrac{3}{5} = \dfrac{}{10}$

f $\dfrac{4}{5} = \dfrac{}{10}$
g $\dfrac{1}{6} = \dfrac{}{12}$
h $\dfrac{5}{6} = \dfrac{}{12}$
i $\dfrac{3}{8} = \dfrac{}{16}$
j $\dfrac{4}{7} = \dfrac{}{14}$

2 Fill in the missing number in each of these equivalent fractions.

a $\dfrac{1}{2} = \dfrac{2}{\underline{}}$
b $\dfrac{1}{8} = \dfrac{2}{\underline{}}$
c $\dfrac{1}{3} = \dfrac{3}{\underline{}}$
d $\dfrac{1}{5} = \dfrac{10}{\underline{}}$
e $\dfrac{1}{8} = \dfrac{5}{\underline{}}$

f $\dfrac{1}{4} = \dfrac{3}{\underline{}}$
g $\dfrac{1}{3} = \dfrac{4}{\underline{}}$
h $\dfrac{1}{5} = \dfrac{5}{\underline{}}$
i $\dfrac{1}{2} = \dfrac{}{6}$
j $\dfrac{1}{5} = \dfrac{}{15}$

k $\dfrac{1}{8} = \dfrac{}{16}$
l $\dfrac{1}{2} = \dfrac{}{10}$
m $\dfrac{1}{4} = \dfrac{}{16}$
n $\dfrac{1}{2} = \dfrac{}{12}$
o $\dfrac{1}{5} = \dfrac{}{25}$

3 Fill in the missing number in each of these equivalent fractions.

a $\dfrac{2}{3} = \dfrac{}{9}$
b $\dfrac{3}{4} = \dfrac{}{8}$
c $\dfrac{4}{5} = \dfrac{8}{\underline{}}$
d $\dfrac{7}{10} = \dfrac{}{20}$
e $\dfrac{3}{5} = \dfrac{9}{\underline{}}$

f $\dfrac{2}{3} = \dfrac{8}{\underline{}}$
g $\dfrac{9}{10} = \dfrac{}{100}$
h $\dfrac{3}{8} = \dfrac{}{24}$
i $\dfrac{5}{6} = \dfrac{25}{\underline{}}$
j $\dfrac{8}{9} = \dfrac{}{27}$

4 Draw lines to match equivalent pairs of fractions.

$\dfrac{2}{8}$ $\dfrac{3}{6}$ $\dfrac{2}{10}$ $\dfrac{10}{12}$ $\dfrac{6}{20}$

$\dfrac{1}{2}$ $\dfrac{1}{5}$ $\dfrac{3}{10}$ $\dfrac{1}{4}$ $\dfrac{5}{6}$

5 Circle all of the fractions that are equivalent to $\dfrac{1}{4}$.

$\dfrac{4}{16}$ $\dfrac{4}{8}$ $\dfrac{2}{8}$ $\dfrac{10}{30}$

$\dfrac{10}{40}$ $\dfrac{8}{20}$ $\dfrac{2}{4}$ $\dfrac{5}{15}$ $\dfrac{5}{20}$

Exercise 5D Fractions of quantities and numbers

This exercise will give you practice in
- finding fractions of numbers and quantities

1 Find half of each of the following quantities.

a 10 cm _____	b 18 g _____	c 20 km _____
d 120 m _____	e 740 cm _____	f 820 mm _____
g 1400 m _____	h 340 g _____	i 62 m _____
j 256 cm _____	k 178 km _____	l 920 mm _____

2 Find a quarter of each of the following quantities.

a 16 km _____	b 20 g _____	c 40 m _____
d 100 mm _____	e 120 kg _____	f 200 cm _____
g 800 g _____	h 60 cm _____	i 48 kg _____
j 360 kg _____	k 880 m _____	l 1200 g _____

3 Find a third of each of the following quantities.

a   9 kg _____   b   21 m _____   c   30 cm _____

d   18 g _____   e   90 cm _____   f   150 km _____

g   300 km _____   h   600 g _____   i   900 mm _____

j   36 kg _____   k   45 m _____   l   1500 m _____

4 How many sixths are there in each of the following whole numbers?

a   6 _____   b   18 _____   c   36 _____   d   48 _____

5 How many eighths are there in each of the following whole numbers?

a   8 _____   b   56 _____   c   80 _____   d   800 _____

Exercise 6A   Mode

This exercise will give you practice in

- making and using a simple database
- finding the mode of a set of data

1 The two tables show test scores for 10 Year 7 students in Maths and English.

Maths	
Darren	9
Navdeep	8
Zarin	6
Hayley	2
Ross	8
Lianne	5
Rahat	5
Jeevan	10
Clinton	8
Tanika	6

English	
Darren	7
Navdeep	10
Zarin	7
Hayley	10
Ross	3
Lianne	6
Rahat	8
Jeevan	7
Clinton	4
Tanika	8

a Complete the database below.

Name	Maths test score	English test score
Darren	9	7
Navdeep	8	

b What is the lowest Maths score?

c   What is the highest English score?

_____

d   Which students scored 8 in the English test?

_____

e   How many students scored more than 6 in the Maths test?

_____

f   Which students did better in the English test than the Maths test?

_____

g   What is the mode for the English test?

_____

h   What is the mode for the Maths test?

_____

2   This database contains information about a group of Year 7 students.

Name	Way of travelling to school	Time to travel to school (minutes)	Distance travelled to school (kilometres)
Charlotte	bus	20	2
Anoop	bus	15	$1\frac{1}{2}$
Peter	cycle	10	1
Amrat	car	15	2
Paula	walk	5	$\frac{1}{2}$
Devan	walk	10	$\frac{1}{2}$
Steven	bus	15	2

a   What is the longest travel time?

_____

b   Which students live $\frac{1}{2}$ km from school?

_____

c   How does Anoop travel to school?

_____

d   What is the most common way of travelling to school?

_____

e i   What is the most common distance travelled? _____

ii   What is this number called? _____

f   What is the mode for the time taken? _____

g   How many students travel for longer than 10 minutes? _____

Exercise 6B   Frequency tables and pictograms

This exercise will give you practice in

  ○ using data from a frequency table to complete a pictogram
  ○ interpreting pictograms and frequency tables

A group of Year 7 students voted for their favourite chocolate bar. The results are shown in the frequency table on the right.

Chocolate bar	Frequency
Snickers	8
Flake	12
Mars Bar	14
Twix	7

1   Complete the pictogram using 😊 to represent two chocolate bars.

Favourite chocolate bar

Snickers

Flake

Mars Bar

Twix   Key: _____

2   How many students voted for Flake?   _____

3   What is the frequency for Twix?   _____

This frequency table shows how many bars of chocolate were eaten in a month by the same Year 7 students.

Chocolate bar	Frequency
Twix	10
Flake	32
Mars Bar	24
Snickers	14

4 Complete the pictogram using ☺ to represent four chocolate bars.

Number of chocolate bars eaten in a month

Twix

Flake

Mars Bar

Snickers

Key: _____

5 How many Snickers were eaten? _____

6 What is the frequency for Mars Bars? _____

Exercise 6C Probability

This exercise will give you practice in
- deciding how certain or likely particular events are

1 Draw a line to match up the words on the left to the ones that mean the same on the right. There may be more than one answer for each!

unlikely	high chance
	no chance
impossible	poor chance
	low chance
certain	must happen
	cannot happen
likely	good chance

2 How likely are these events to happen? Write the correct word next to each event.

unlikely   impossible   certain   likely

a   You will hand all of your homework in on time _____

b   You will win the Lottery if you buy a ticket _____

c   You will get older _____

d   This lesson will end _____

e   You will be in Year 11 next year _____

f   You will win X Factor 2012 if you enter _____

3 Look at these events.

A   You will be one year older next year

B   You will grow another head

C   You will meet David Beckham

D   You will see your form tutor next week

Place the letter for each of the events where you think it should go on this scale.

no chance   poor chance   good chance   certain

Exercise 6D   Bar charts 1

This exercise will give you practice in

• solving problems by representing data in and reading data from a bar chart

Sally and Tim surveyed their class on eye colour. They recorded their results in the tally chart on the right.

1 Fill in the frequency column.

Eye Colour	Tally	Frequency
Blue	‖‖‖ |||	
Green	‖‖‖ ||	
Brown	‖‖‖ ‖‖‖		
Grey	||	
Other			

2 Complete the bar chart.

3 How many students have green eyes?

_____

4 Which is the most common eye colour?

_____

5 How many students were surveyed in total?

_____

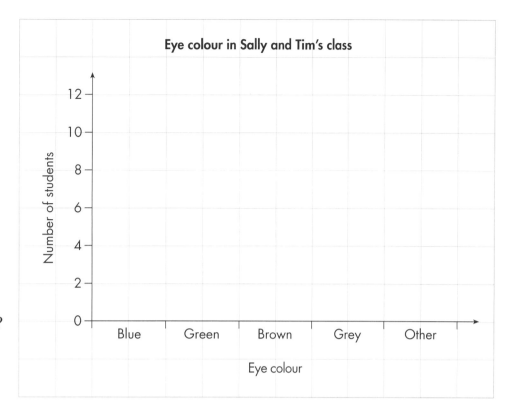

Eye colour in Sally and Tim's class

Exercise 6E   Bar charts 2

This exercise will give you practice in

- solving problems by representing data in and reading data from a bar chart

Alex asked six of his friends how much television they had watched, in minutes, one evening. The results are shown in the frequency table on the right.

Name	Amount of television watched (minutes)
Raj	20
Stephan	75
Kylie	30
Gemma	20
Sunil	0
Craig	60

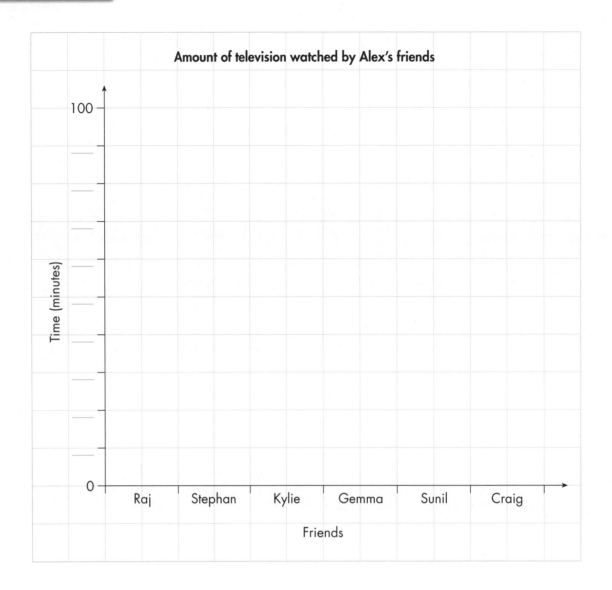

Amount of television watched by Alex's friends

Time (minutes)

100

0

Raj   Stephan   Kylie   Gemma   Sunil   Craig

Friends

1. Write in the scale for time in the spaces provided.

2. Complete the bar chart using the data in the frequency table.

3. Who watched the most television? _____

4. Who watched the least television? _____

5. What is the most common amount of television watched? _____

6. What is the answer to **Question 5** called? _____

Exercise 7A Decimals–tenths

This exercise will give you practice in

- using decimal notation for tenths
- ordering decimal fractions with one decimal place

1 Write the tenths from 0 to 1 as decimal fractions.

0   0.1   0.2   1

2 Fill in the missing numbers on the number lines. The first one has been done for you.

a 8.6   8.7   8.8   8.9   9.0   9.1   9.2   9.3   9.4   9.5   9.6

b 5.5   6.5

c 3.2   4.2

d 29.6   30.6

e 31.4   32.4

f 43.2   44.2

3 Order these groups of decimal fractions from the smallest to the largest.

a 6.3   7.3   2.6   5.6   7.6   _____

b 6.8   9.2   9.7   5.2   5.8   _____

c 14.8   13.6   14   13   14.3   _____

d 78.1   87.2   78.3   87.4   88.2   _____

e 22.6   26.7   25.1   23.2   28.1   _____

f 22.6   22.5   19.2   20.1   28.2   _____

Exercise 7B Decimals-hundredths

This exercise will give you practice in

- using decimal notation for tenths and hundredths
- ordering decimal fractions with the same number of decimal places

1 Write the hundredths from 0 to 0.1 as decimal fractions.

0   0.01   0.02   0.1

2 Fill in missing numbers on the number lines. The first one has been done for you.

a 8.4 *8.41 8.42 8.43 8.44 8.45 8.46 8.47 8.48 8.49* 8.5

b 5.5 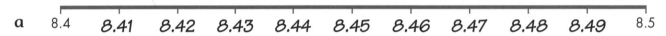 5.6

c 31.4  31.5

d 5.5  5.6

e 42.3  42.4

f 18  18.1

3 Order these groups of decimal fractions from smallest to largest.

a 7.56   7.65   7.55   7.60   7.50   _____

b 18.03   19.30   19.04   20.15   18.40   _____

c 27.34   27.65   27.56   27.43   27.50   _____

d 46.02   46.09   64.23   46.29   46.12   _____

e 33.88   33.77   33.99   33.66   33.55   _____

f 22.34   22.43   22.36   22.63   22.90   _____

Exercise 7C   Rounding decimals

This exercise will give you practice in

- rounding decimals with one or two decimal places to the nearest integer

1 Write down the two whole numbers that each decimal comes between. Circle the number that the decimal is closest to. The first one has been done for you.

a _6_   6.8   (7)   b _____   5.2   _____

c _____   3.6   _____   d _____   4.9   _____

e _____   5.5   _____   f _____   23.2   _____

g _____   19.6   _____   h _____   1.2   _____

i _____   7.5   _____   j _____   3.23   _____

k _____   17.51   _____   l _____   34.76   _____

2 Using the digit cards below, write down 10 numbers to one or two decimal places. Then round them to the nearest whole number.

_____ _____   _____ _____

_____ _____   _____ _____

_____ _____   _____ _____

_____ _____   _____ _____

Exercise 7D   Equivalence

This exercise will give you practice in
- converting between fractions and decimals

1 Draw lines to join a decimal to the correct fraction.

0.5	$\frac{1}{10}$
0.1	$\frac{8}{10}$
0.8	$\frac{3}{10}$
0.25	$\frac{1}{2}$
0.6	$\frac{9}{10}$
0.9	$\frac{6}{10}$
0.3	$\frac{4}{10}$
0.75	$\frac{3}{4}$
0.4	$\frac{1}{4}$

2 Convert these decimals to mixed numbers.

a 2.1 _____

b 9.2 _____

c 8.4 _____

d 5.6 _____

e 7.3 _____

f 4.9 _____

g 5.5 _____

h 1.7 _____

i 3.8 _____

3 Convert these mixed numbers to decimals.

a $22\frac{2}{10}$ _____

b $33\frac{3}{10}$ _____

c $25\frac{5}{10}$ _____

d $12\frac{1}{2}$ _____

e $15\frac{1}{4}$ _____

Exercise 7E Solving problems

This exercise will give you practice in

- solving problems involving decimals

Year 7 is selling tickets for the end of term concert. Each ticket costs £2.50. The hall can hold up to 500 people. How much money will the school make if the hall is full on the day of the concert?

Problem

Calculation

Answer to calculation

Answer to problem

Exercise 8A   Angles

This exercise will give you practice in
- identifying obtuse, acute and right angles
- beginning to apply these terms to triangles

1 Circle the lines that form angles.

a    b    c    d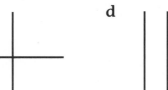

2 In what unit do we measure angles? _____

3 Circle the acute angles.

a    b    c    d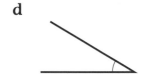

4 Circle the obtuse angles.

a 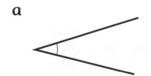   b    c    d

5 Circle the right angles.

a    b 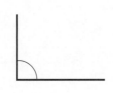   c 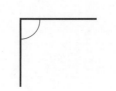   d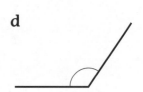

6 In the spaces provided, write down which angle in each of the triangles is an obtuse angle, an acute angle or a right angle. Remember that some triangles may not contain any obtuse angles or right angles!

a 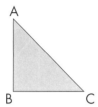   b    c 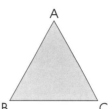   d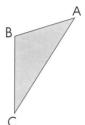

obtuse angle: _____   _____   _____   _____

acute angle: _____   _____   _____   _____

right angle: _____   _____   _____   _____

Exercise 8B Classifying triangles

This exercise will give you practice in

○ classifying triangles according to the properties of their sides and angles

1 a, b, c and d are four isosceles triangles. Circle the two angles that are the same in each triangle.

a    b 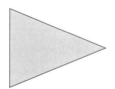   c    d

2 Which of these triangles are isosceles triangles?

a    b   c   d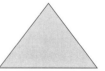

3 Which of the triangles below are scalene triangles?

a　　　　　　　　b　　　　　　　　c　　　　　　　　d

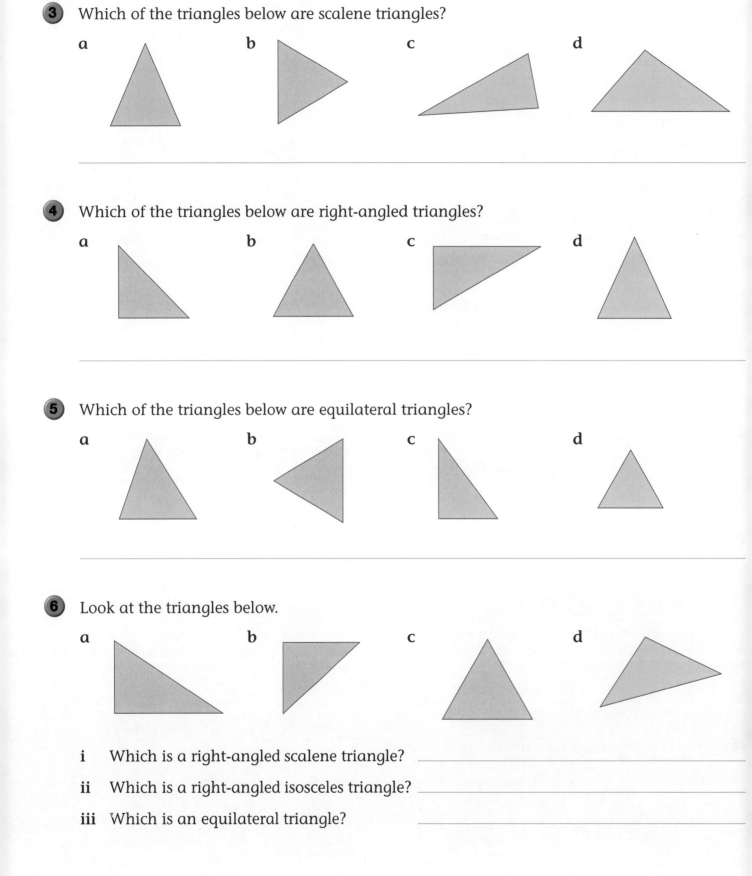

4 Which of the triangles below are right-angled triangles?

a　　　　　　　　b　　　　　　　　c　　　　　　　　d

5 Which of the triangles below are equilateral triangles?

a　　　　　　　　b　　　　　　　　c　　　　　　　　d

6 Look at the triangles below.

a　　　　　　　　b　　　　　　　　c　　　　　　　　d

i   Which is a right-angled scalene triangle? _____

ii   Which is a right-angled isosceles triangle? _____

iii Which is an equilateral triangle? _____

7 Draw in any lines of symmetry for each of the following triangles.

a   b   c   d

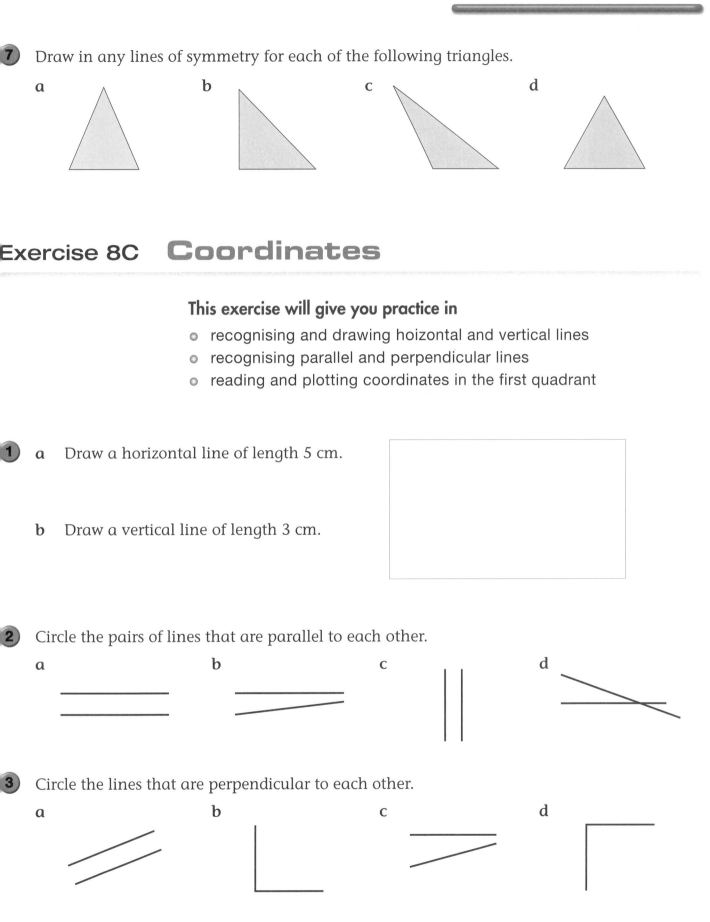

Exercise 8C Coordinates

This exercise will give you practice in

- recognising and drawing hoizontal and vertical lines
- recognising parallel and perpendicular lines
- reading and plotting coordinates in the first quadrant

1 a Draw a horizontal line of length 5 cm.

   b Draw a vertical line of length 3 cm.

2 Circle the pairs of lines that are parallel to each other.

a   b   c   d

3 Circle the lines that are perpendicular to each other.

a   b   c   d

4 For each of the sets of lines shown (**a**, **b**, **c** and **d**), write down whether each of the statements is true (T) or false (F).

a   b   c   d

		a	b	c	d
i	These lines are horizontal and parallel to each other.				
ii	These lines are horizontal.				
iii	These lines are parallel.				
iv	These lines are perpendicular to each other.				

5 **a** Write in x and y in the spaces on the grid to show which is the x-axis and which is the y-axis.

b Place an X at the origin (0, 0)

c On the grid plot the following points.
A(0, 1) B(1, 5) C(3, 5) D(3, 7) E(4, 2)

d On your grid, join the two points that make a horizontal line.

e On your grid, join the two points that make a vertical line.

f Are your two lines perpendicular to each other?

_____

g Draw a line on your grid to make a triangle.

h What sort of triangle have you drawn?

_____

Exercise 9A   **Tally charts and frequency tables**

This exercise will give you practice in

- creating and using tally charts and frequency tables

The table below shows a survey of the type of television programmes a group of Year 12 students enjoy most.

Type of programme	Tally	Frequency
Soap operas	$\cancel{||||}$ $\cancel{||||}$ $\cancel{||||}$ $\cancel{||||}$ $\cancel{||||}$ $|||$	
Comedy	$\cancel{||||}$ $\cancel{||||}$ $|||$	
The news	$\cancel{||||}$ $||$	
Reality TV	$\cancel{||||}$ $\cancel{||||}$ $\cancel{||||}$	
Drama	$\cancel{||||}$ $\cancel{||||}$ $|$	
Documentaries	$\cancel{||||}$ $\cancel{||||}$ $||$	

1 Count up the tally marks and fill in the frequency column.

2 **a** Which is the most popular type of programme? _____

 b How many people voted for this? _____

3 **a** Which is the least popular type of programme? _____

 b How many people voted for this? _____

4 How many people enjoy drama programmes the most? _____

5 How many people enjoy comedy programmes the most? _____

6 How many more people chose soap operas than drama as their favourite type of programme? _____

Exercise 9B Mode and range

This exercise will give you practice in

- finding the mode and range for a set of data

1 Twenty people were stopped in the street and asked their age. The results are shown below.

15, 27, 30, 56, 72, 30, 42, 17, 21, 64, 30, 17, 36, 39, 19, 30, 41, 43, 22, 53

a Place the ages in order from youngest to eldest. (You may want to use a pencil!)

_____

_____

b What is the mode of the ages? _____

c What is the range of the ages? _____

2 Find the mode and range for both of the following sets of data, sorting the data first.

a 2, 5, 6, 8, 8, 6, 7, 7, 4, 9, 1, 1, 3, 2, 4, 8, 9, 8

Sort the data: _____

_____

Mode: _____ Range: _____

b 23, 22, 28, 21, 21, 29, 22, 25, 24, 22, 27, 28

Sort the data: _____

_____

Mode: _____ Range: _____

3 The database shows some of the results of the school tennis club.

Name	Won	Lost	Drawn
Sharon	2	1	3
Sophie	4	0	0
Keon	3	1	0
Raj	2	1	1
Joely	2	0	2
Jack	3	1	1
Angela	1	3	0
Steven	1	2	1

a How many games did Keon lose? _____

b How many games did Sophie win? _____

c How many games did Angela draw? _____

d What is the mode for the number of games lost? _____

e What is the mode for the number of games won? _____

f What was the total number of games lost? _____

g Which two players won and lost the same number of games? _____

Exercise 9C Carroll diagrams

This exercise will give you practice in

○ putting data into Carroll diagrams and using it to solve problems

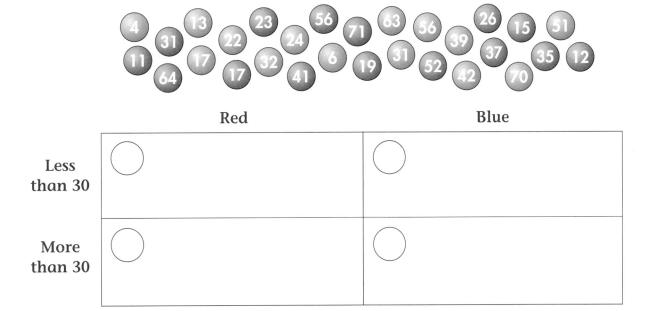

a Write each number in the correct space on the Carroll diagram.

b Count the numbers in each space on the Carroll diagram. Write the totals in the circle.

c How many numbers are 30 or more? _____

d How many blue numbers are less than 30? _____

e How many reds are there all together? _____

	Odd	Even
Between 20 and 50	◯	◯
Not between 20 and 50	◯	◯

2 Look at the numbers again.

a Write each number in the correct space on this Carroll diagram.

b Count the numbers in each space on the Carroll diagram. Write the totals in the circle.

c How many odd numbers are there? _____

d How many numbers are between 20 and 50? _____

e How many even numbers are between 20 and 50? _____

f How many odd numbers are not between 20 and 50? _____

Exercise 9D Bar-line charts

This exercise will give you practice in

- using data from tally charts and frequency tables to complete bar-line charts
- reading data from bar-line charts

Navdeep recorded the number of different coloured cars that drove past her house one Saturday afternoon for a school project. She recorded her results in a tally chart.

Colour	Number of cars	Frequency
Red	ⅢⅢ IIII	
Black	ⅢⅢ ⅢⅢ III	
Blue	ⅢⅢ II	
Silver	III	
Green	ⅢⅢ	
White	ⅢⅢ III	

Write the frequencies on the table.

Complete the bar-line chart.

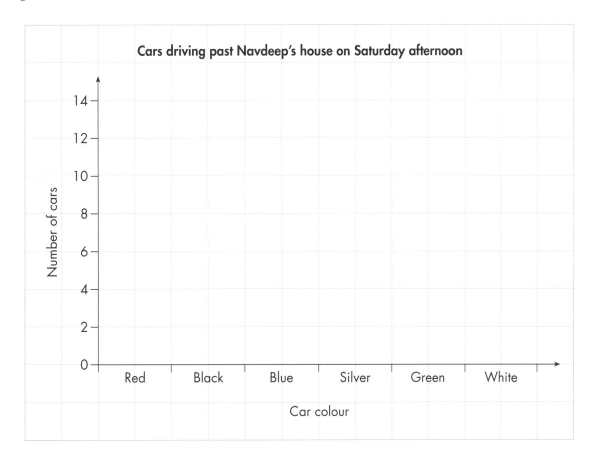

Which colour car drove past Navdeep's house the most? _____

What is this number called? _____

How many blue cars drove past Navdeep's house? _____

How many cars drove past Navdeep's house in total? _____

How many of the cars that drove past Navdeep's house were not black? _____

Exercise 10A Multiplication

This exercise will give you practice in

○ using and learning multiplication facts

1 Complete each of the following calculations.

a $7 \times 4 =$ _____

b $4 \times 9 =$ _____

c $7 \times 3 =$ _____

d $4 \times 6 =$ _____

e $7 \times 9 =$ _____

f $8 \times 6 =$ _____

g $9 \times 8 =$ _____

h _____ $\times 6 = 42$

i $5 \times$ _____ $= 45$

j $8 \times$ _____ $= 56$

k _____ $\times$ _____ $= 24$

l _____ $\times$ _____ $= 48$

m _____ $\times$ _____ $= 36$

2 Some of these calculations are incorrect. Work out each multiplication and circle those that are incorrect.

$2 \times 40 = 100$ _____ $3 \times 40 = 120$ _____ $4 \times 50 = 250$ _____ $5 \times 20 = 100$ _____

$6 \times 20 = 120$ _____ $5 \times 50 = 250$ _____ $3 \times 30 = 80$ _____

$6 \times 40 = 240$ _____ $3 \times 50 = 150$ _____

$7 \times 20 = 150$ _____ $4 \times 80 = 320$ _____ $5 \times 40 = 200$ _____

$6 \times 30 = 160$ _____

3 Complete the multiplication grid.

×	4	8	1	10
3	12	24	3	30
8				
6		48		
9				90
5	20		5	
1				
7				

Exercise 10B Division

This exercise will give you practice in

- using and learning division facts

1 Complete each of the following calculations.

a $32 \div 8 =$ _____

b $24 \div 4 =$ _____

c $27 \div 3 =$ _____

d $56 \div 7 =$ _____

e $72 \div 8 =$ _____

f $30 \div 5 =$ _____

g $80 \div 10 =$ _____

h $60 \div 5 =$ _____

i _____ $\div 3 = 5$

j $24 \div$ _____ $= 4$

k $32 \div$ _____ $= 8$

l $64 \div$ _____ $= 8$

m $54 \div$ _____ $= 6$

2 Work out the division facts. Draw a line to the matching multiplication fact.

a $24 \div 6 =$ _____ 4×8

b $32 \div 4 =$ _____ 9×3

c $27 \div 3 =$ _____ 4×4

d $20 \div 4 =$ _____ 3×6

e $18 \div 6 =$ _____ 7×4

f $16 \div 4 =$ _____ 6×4

g $28 \div 7 =$ _____ 5×4

Exercise 10C Brackets

This exercise will give you practice in

○ using brackets in calculations

① Complete the table below by following the example given and the steps below.

- write the number sentence in the first column
- decide which order to complete the calculations
- write the calculations in the order you do them
- work out the answer

An example

	Number sentence	First calculation	Next calculation	Answer
Example	$(3 + 6) \times 5$	$3 + 6 = 9$	9×5	45
a				
b				
c				
d				
e				
f				
g				
h				

a $3 \times (2 + 5)$ b $(17 + 23) \div 4$ c $35 \div (5 + 2)$ d $(4 + 2) \times 5$

e $(10 + 14) \div 3$ f $14 \div (2 + 5)$ g $7 \times (6 - 4)$ h $(8 - 4) \div 2$

② Put in the brackets to make these calculations correct.

a $3 \times 40 - 20 = 60$ b $5 \times 20 \div 10 = 10$ c $3 + 6 - 1 \div 4 = 2$

d $32 + 8 \div 4 = 10$ e $36 \div 6 - 3 = 12$ f $5 \times 5 + 8 = 65$

Exercise 10D BODMAS

This exercise will give you practice in

○ using BODMAS, the order of operations

1 Write the short form for the following square numbers.

a 3×3 _____

b 4×4 _____

c 5×5 _____

d 6×6 _____

e 7×7 _____

f 8×8 _____

2 Complete the table below by following the example given and the steps below.
- write the number sentence in the first column
- decide which order to complete the calculations
- write the calculations in the order you do them
- work out the answer

	Number sentence	First calculation	Next calculation	Next calculation	Answer
Example	$5 + 3 \times 4 + 2^2$	$2^2 = 4$	$3 \times 4 = 12$	$5 + 12 + 4$	21
a					
b					
c					
d					
e					
f					
g					
h					
i					

a $6 + 4 \times 6 + 3^2$

b $2^2 + 17 + 24 \div 4$

c $35 \div 5 + 7 + 3^2$

d $4 + 2^2 \times 2$

e $(10 + 14) \div 3 + 5^2$

f $10 + 4 \div 2 + 3^2$

g $4 \times 3 - 5 + 5^2$

h $19 + (10 - 4) \times 6$

i $(30 - 8) \div 2 + 4$

Exercise 10E Partitioning

This exercise will give you practice in

o partitioning techniques for adding and subtracting two-digit numbers in your head

1 Add each pair of numbers together. First add the tens and then the units. Write down your method as a calculation. The first one has been done for you.

a 47 21

$40 + 20 = 60$
$7 + 1 = 8$
$60 + 8 = 68$

b 57 35

c 62 32

d 76 54

e 47 34

f 56 32

g 72 41

h 88 33

i 96 21

2 Now find the difference between each pair of numbers. First subtract the tens and then the units.

a 47 – 21

b 57 – 35

c 62 – 32

d 76 – 54

e   47 – 34

f   56 – 32

g   72 – 41

h   88 – 33

i   96 – 21

3 Write five addition calculations and five subtraction calculations using the numbers below. First work them out in your head and then write down the calculations.

56   74   68   32   41   89   52   23   17   66   43   75   61

Exercise 10F Greater or less than

This exercise will give you practice in

- using the symbols <, >, ≥, ≤ and =

<	>	≥	≤	=
less than	greater than	greater than or equal to	less than or equal to	equal to

1 Write <, > or = between each pair of numbers to make a true statement.

   a 156 ____ 166   **b** 178 ____ 134   **c** 198 ____ 230

   d 144 ____ 144   **e** 451 ____ 667   **f** 656 ____ 774

   g 886 ____ 886   **h** 155 ____ 166   **i** 187 ____ 234

2 Write <, > or = between each pair of numbers to make a true statement.

   a 1156 ____ 2570   **b** 1780 ____ 1340   **c** 2190 ____ 2300

   d 7899 ____ 8798   **e** 3456 ____ 3657   **f** 7543 ____ 7421

   g 9754 ____ 9734   **h** 13 564 ____ 25 654   **i** 18 765 ____ 18 640

3 Write <, > or = between each pair of numbers to make a true statement.

   a 11.43 ____ 23.54   **b** 16.56 ____ 16.56   **c** 17.89 ____ 14.32

   d 21.34 ____ 36.98   **e** 54.32 ____ 56.51   **f** 87.22 ____ 93.45

   g 56.16 ____ 56.16   **h** 65.73 ____ 88.24   **i** 16.42 ____ 14.62

4 Circle the numbers in the box that are ≤ 175.

Put a line through the numbers in the box that are ≥ 150.

Which numbers have you both circled and put a line through?

175	90
180	30
40	1 163
300	174
70	200

5 Circle the numbers in the box that are ≥ 45.

Put a line through the numbers in the box that are ≤ 68.

Which numbers have you both circled and put a line through?

71	40	68
	45	44
	19	
317		30
94	84	701

Exercise 11A Doubling and halving

This exercise will give you practice in
- doubling and halving in calculations

1 Double each of the following numbers.

24	62	34	66	55	28	72	80	45

2 Halve each of the following numbers.

128	136	150	144	194	156	178	182

3 The rule for $\times 50$ is first $\times 100$ then $\div 2$. Use this rule to calculate the answer to each of the following questions. The first one has been done for you.

a 18×50

$(18 \times 100) \div 2 = 1800 \div 2 = 900$

b 26×50

c 44×50

d 14×50

e 37×50

f 46×50

g 16×50

h 19×50

i 34×50

j 29×50

Exercise 11B Estimation

This exercise will give you practice in

- rounding integers to the nearest 10
- rounding decimals to the nearest integer
- estimating calculations by approximation

1 Write the approximation to the nearest 10 for each of the following numbers. The first one has been done for you.

a 154 *154 ≈ 150*   b 122 _____   c 166 _____

d 235 _____   e 288 _____   f 299 _____

g 323 _____   h 355 _____   i 363 _____

j 402 _____   k 408 _____   l 555 _____

m 582 _____

2 Write the approximation to the nearest whole number for each of the following.

a 23.24 _____   b 21.55 _____   c 44.87 _____

d 32.43 _____   e 55.47 _____   f 56.54 _____

g 77.29 _____   h 83.57 _____   i 89.99 _____

j 91.24 _____   k 94.11 _____   l 96.52 _____

m 98.38 _____

3 Approximate the answer to each calculation. The first one has been done for you.

a 37×19 *37 × 19 ≈ 40 × 20 = 800*   b 12×29 _____

c 22×38 _____   d 34×17 _____

e 42×44 _____   f 14×45 _____

g 38×48 _____

4 Check your approximations in **Question 3** by working out the answers using your calculator.

a _____   b _____   c _____   d _____

e _____   f _____   g _____

Exercise 11C Rounding after division

This exercise will give you practice in

- finding remainders after division
- using division to solve word problems
- rounding up or down after division

1 Find the answers to these division problems. Work out your answers on rough paper and write the answer in the box. Watch out – some of them have remainders!

a $24 \div 3$ ☐   b $32 \div 4$ ☐

c $42 \div 5$ ☐   d $54 \div 9$ ☐

e $36 \div 9$ ☐   f $47 \div 4$ ☐

g $72 \div 8$ ☐   h $25 \div 3$ ☐

i $16 \div 2$ ☐   j $43 \div 4$ ☐

2 The Big Dipper seats 8 people per carriage. There are 240 people in the queue. How many carriages will be needed?

3 Bread rolls are sold in packs of 6. A batch of dough makes 128 bread rolls. How many packs of bread rolls can be made up out of 1 batch of dough?

4 Class 7A are going on a school trip in minibuses. There are 37 students in Class 7A and each minibus can hold 8 students. How many minibuses will be needed?

Exercise 11D Solving money problems

This exercise will give you practice in

- using division to solve real-life problems involving money

1 Divide these amounts in pounds by the numbers given. Give your answers in pence.

    a £1 ÷ 2 _____   **b** £1 ÷ 4 _____   **c** £1 ÷ 10 _____

    d £4 ÷ 5 _____   **e** £3 ÷ 4 _____   **f** £2 ÷ 5 _____

    g £5 ÷ 10 _____

2 Five Year 7 classes were given £200 by the head teacher to spend on their Christmas party. How much did each class receive? Show your working.

_____

_____

_____

3 Four friends went out carol singing and collected £17. If they shared the money equally between them, how much did each one receive? Show your working.

_____

_____

_____

4 Three local businesses donated a total of £61.50 to a school. Given that each business donated the same amount, how much did each donate? Show your working.

_____

_____

_____

5 The ICT department bought six identical printer cartridges at a total cost of £37.50. How much did each cartridge cost?

_____

_____

Exercise 11E   More money problems

This exercise will give you practice in

- using multiplication and addition to solve real-life problems involving money

1 Use your calculator to find the total cost of each set of items. Write down your calculation

a   two pairs of trainers and an MP3 player

b   two mobile phones and three pairs of trainers

c   three MP3 players, a pair of trainers and a micro system

d   three pairs of trainers, two MP3 players and a mobile phone

2 Use your calculator to find the total cost of each set of items. Write down your calculation.

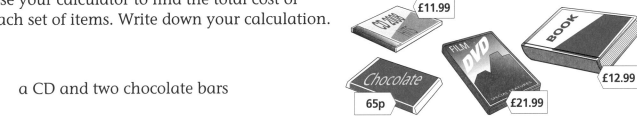

a   a CD and two chocolate bars

b   two CDs and two DVDs

c   five CDs, two books and a chocolate bar

d   two DVDs, three CDs and two chocolate bars

e   three of each item

3 Using the information from **Question 2**, answer each of the following questions.

    a How much more does a DVD cost than a book?

    _____

    b How much more does a book cost than ten chocolate bars?

    _____

    c How much more does it cost to buy two CDs rather than one DVD?

    _____

    d How much more do two DVDs cost than two CDs?

    _____

Exercise 12A Classifying and ordering angles

This exercise will give you practice in

- identifing and ordering acute, obtuse and reflex angles

1 Circle the acute angles.

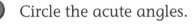

2 Circle the obtuse angles.

3 Circle the reflex angles.

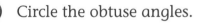

4 Write down the order of these acute angles from smallest to largest.

a   b   c   d

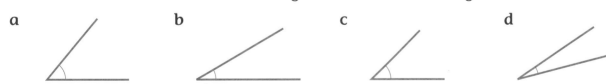

5 Write down the order of these obtuse angles from smallest to largest.

a   b   c   d

6 Write down the order of these reflex angles from smallest to largest.

a   b   c   d

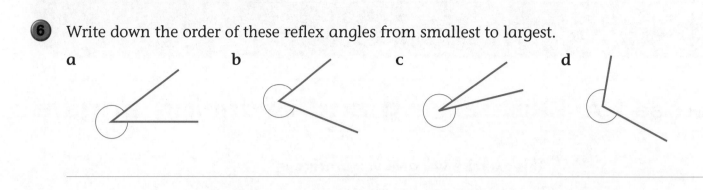

Exercise 12B Measuring and drawing angles

This exercise will give you practice in
- measuring and drawing angles using a protractor

1 Using a protractor, measure these acute angles.

a   b

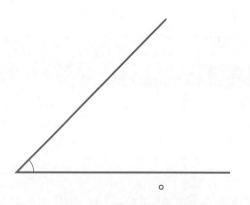

°
_____

°
_____

c   d

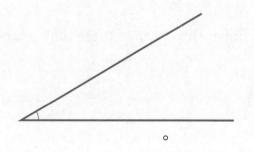

°
_____

°
_____

2 Using a protractor, measure these obtuse angles.

a

°
_____

b

°
_____

c

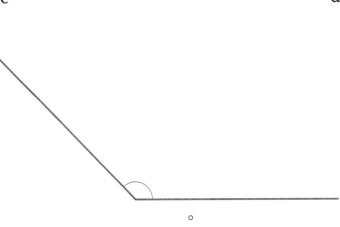

°
_____

d

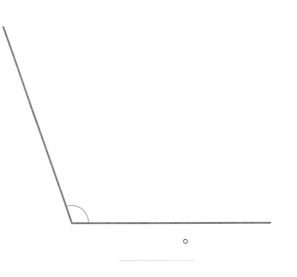

°
_____

3 Starting from the left-hand side of the line, draw the following angles and write down if they are acute or obtuse.

a   45°   b   60°   c   120°   d   160°

a   _____   b   _____

_____   _____

c _____

d _____

4 Starting from the right-hand side of the line, draw the following angles and write down if they are acute or obtuse.

a 130° **b** 30° **c** 70° **d** 100°

a _____

b _____

c _____

d _____

Exercise 12C Solving geometric problems

This exercise will give you practice in

- recognising properties of rectangles and other quadrilaterals, such as parallel sides and right angles

Some of the sides and diagonals are missing from these shapes.

a
b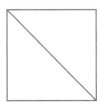
c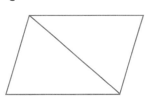
d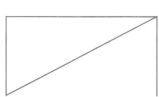

e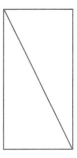
f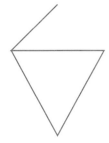
g
h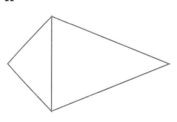

1 Complete the shapes and draw in any missing diagonals.

2 Mark in the right angles on the shapes.

3 Which shapes do not have four right angles? _____

4 Which shapes are rectangles? _____

5 Which shapes are squares? _____

6 Which shapes do not have any parallel lines? _____

Exercise 13A **Percentages**

This exercise will give you practice in

○ understanding and using percentages

1 Look at the grids and write down what fraction and what percentage of each grid is shaded.

a
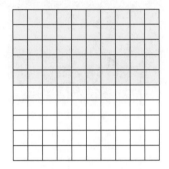

b
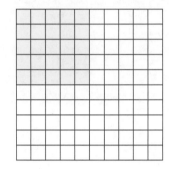

c
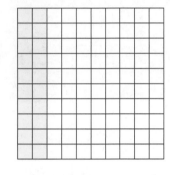

d
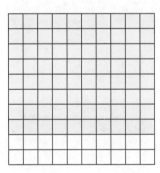

e
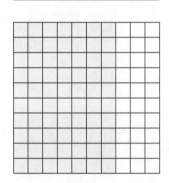

f
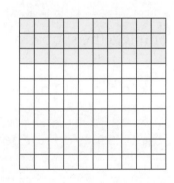

g
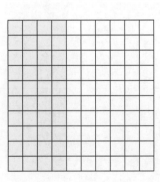

h
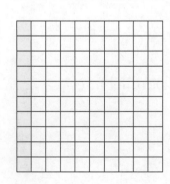

i
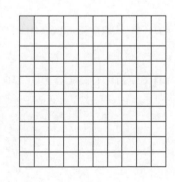

Exercise 13B Percentages of quantities

This exercise will give you practice in

○ finding percentages of whole number quantities

1 Solve the percentage problems.

a   I eat 50% of my pizza. What percentage is left?

b   70% of Year 7 students travel to school by bus? What percentage do not travel to school by bus?

c   If 90% of your homework was correct, what percentage did you get wrong?

2 Work out each of the following. Show your working.

a   50% of 100 kg

b   50% of £10

c   50% of 10 cm

d   50% of £1

e   50% of 10 mm

f   25% of £1

g   25% of 100 kg

h   25% of 10 cm

i   10% of 100 kg

j   10% of £1

k   10% of 10 mm

3 Work out each of the following. Show your working.

a   50% of £30

b   50% of 150 m

c   50% of £22

d   25% of £40

e   25% of 60 kg _____

f   25% of £20 _____

g   10% of £160 _____

h   10% of 180 cm _____

i   10% of £50 _____

Exercise 13C Ratio and proportion

This exercise will give you practice in

- using ratio and proportion

1 Complete each of the following tables.

a   For every £1 that James spends on holiday, his sister, Claire spends £4. Complete the table showing how much they spend.

James	Claire
£1	£4
£2	

b   For every two boys in the class, there are three girls. Complete the table showing the boys and girls in the class.

Boys	Girls
2	3
4	

c   For every two apples that Eddie eats, Jill eats four. Complete the table showing how many apples they eat.

Eddie	Jill
2	4
4	

2 The wine gums I buy always have two orange ones for every four red ones.

Orange	Red
2	4

a Complete the table for the number of red and orange wine gums.

b What is the ratio of orange wine gums to red wine gums?

c How many red wine gums would I have eaten if I had eaten 14 orange wine gums?

d How many orange wine gums would I have eaten if I had eaten 28 red wine gums?

Exercise 13D Solving problems with ratio and proportion

This exercise will give you practice in

○ using ratio and proportion to solve problems

1 Complete the tables to help you solve the problems.

a Raj's mum made 16 cakes. For every cake Raj ate, his mum ate 3.

Raj	Raj's mum	Total cakes
1	3	4

i How many cakes did Raj eat?

ii How many cakes did his mum eat?

b A family drinks one glass of still water for every two glasses of fizzy water. One weekend they drank 21 glasses of water.

Still water	Fizzy water	Total water
1	2	3

i How many glasses of still water did they drink?

_____

ii How many glasses of fizzy water did they drink?

_____

2 Work out the problems using the proportions given. You may want to draw a table on rough paper to help you.

a Every box of Meltos chocolates has three milk chocolate Meltos for every four plain chocolate Meltos. A box contains 49 Meltos.

i How many milk chocolate Meltos are in a box? _____

ii How many plain chocolate Meltos are in a box? _____

b A bag of mixed grapes contains three green grapes for every five black grapes. A bag normally contains 48 grapes.

i How many green grapes are there in a bag? _____

ii How many black grapes are there? _____

Exercise 14A More multiplication

This exercise will give you practice in

- learning and using multiplication facts up to 10 × 10

You should know your times tables up to 10 × 10 already, but you can check your answers on the multiplication square.

1	2	3	4	5	6	7	8	9	10
2	4	6	8	10	12	14	16	18	20
3	6	9	12	15	18	21	24	27	30
4	8	12	16	20	24	28	32	36	40
5	10	15	20	25	30	35	40	45	50
6	12	18	24	30	36	42	48	54	60
7	14	21	28	35	42	49	56	63	70
8	16	24	32	40	48	56	64	72	80
9	18	27	36	45	54	63	72	81	90
10	20	30	40	50	60	70	80	90	100

1 Answer these either using mental methods or by using the multiplication square.

a 7 × 9 _____   **b** 9 × 8 _____

c 6 × 8 _____   **d** 7 × 4 _____

e 9 × 5 _____   **f** 7 × 6 _____

g 8 × 4 _____   **h** 9 × 3 _____

i 9 × 9 _____

2 Write down all the multiplication facts for each of the following numbers.

a 32 _____

b 24 _____

c 40 _____

d 54 _____

e 36 _____

3 Complete the multiplication grids.

a

×	2	4	6	8
2	4	8	12	16
3				
7				56
8		32		

b

×	3	5	7	9
6		30		
5				45
4	12			
3			21	

Exercise 14B Factor trees

This exercise will give you practice in

- finding pairs of factors of any numbers up to 100 using factor trees

1 For each set of numbers multiply one number by the other number to find the product. The first one has been done for you.

a 3 5

b 4 6
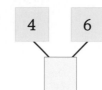

c 8 8

d 5 2
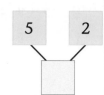

2 Write down the missing factors.

a
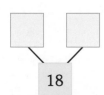
18

b

32

c
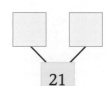
21

d
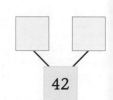
42

3 Build your own factor tree. Use the numbers below to start.

a 2 2 3 2
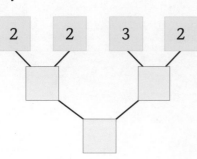

b 2 2 2 2
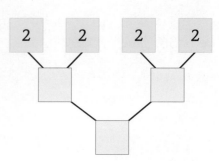

c

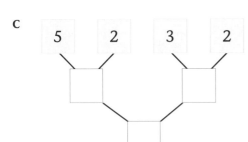

d

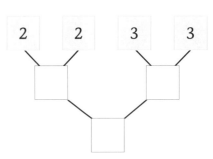

e

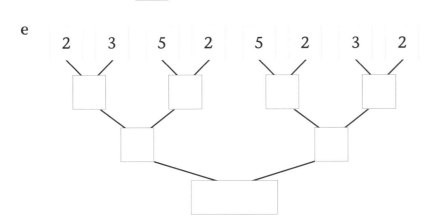

f

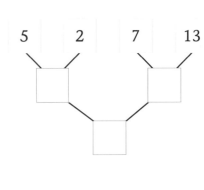

Exercise 15A **Symmetry**

This exercise will give you practice in

- recognising lines of symmetry in shapes

You may use a mirror to help you in this exercise.

1 These shapes all have one line of symmetry. Draw the dotted line of symmetry on each shape.

   a   b   c   d   e

2 Some of these shapes do not have reflective symmetry.
Put a tick inside the shapes that do not have reflective symmetry.

   a   b   c   d

3 Mark any lines of symmetry with a dotted line in each of the following shapes. Don't forget to use a ruler.

   a   b   c   d   e

Exercise 15B Reflections

This exercise will give you practice in

○ reflecting a shape in a mirror line

1) Complete each of the half-shapes below by reflecting them in the mirror lines marked.

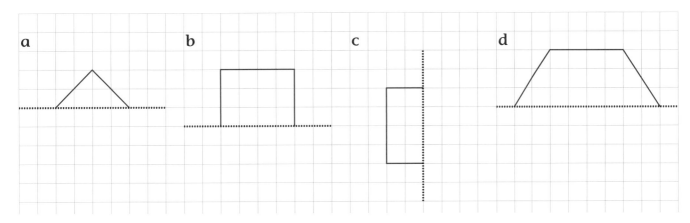

2) Reflect each of the following shapes in the mirror lines shown.

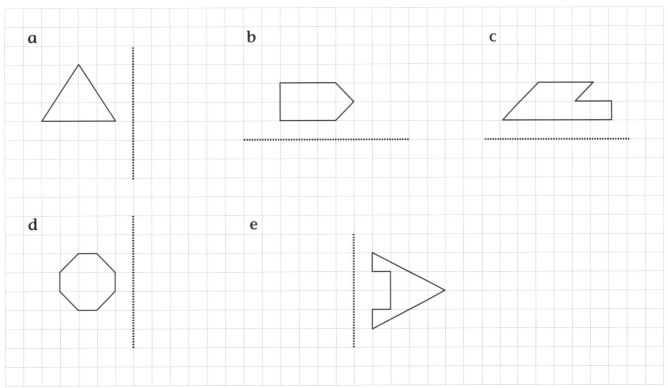

Exercise 15C **Symmetrical patterns**

This exercise will give you practice in

- completing symmetrical patterns with two lines of symmetry at right angles

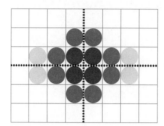

1 Check that the pattern above has two lines of symmetry. Place your mirror on the dotted lines.

2 Complete each pattern by reflecting it in both the horizontal and vertical axes of symmetry. Remember to check your reflections with a mirror.

a

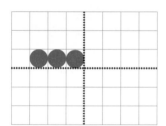

b

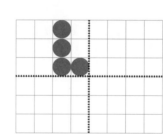

c

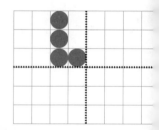

3 Complete each pattern by reflecting it in both the horizontal and vertical axes of symmetry. Remember to check your reflections with a mirror.

a

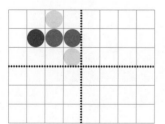

b

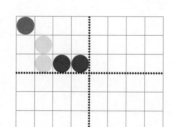

c

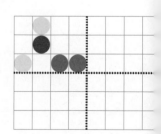

Exercise 15D Translations

This exercise will give you practice in

○ recognising where a shape will be after a translation

1 **a** Write down the coordinates for shape A in the space below.

(___, ___), (___, ___), (___, ___), (___, ___)

b Write down the coordinates for shape B in the space below.

(___, ___), (___, ___), (___, ___), (___, ___)

c Complete the sentence.

Shape ___ has been translated ___ units to the right to make shape B.

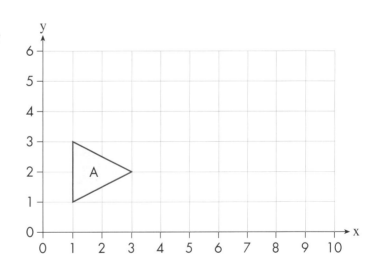

2 **a** Write down the coordinates for shape A in the space below.

(___, ___), (___, ___), (___, ___)

b **i** Add four units to the first number in shape A's coordinates to make shape B and draw this on the grid.

ii The coordinates for shape B are

(___, ___), (___, ___), (___, ___).

c **i** Add six units to the first number in shape A's coordinates to make shape C.

ii The coordinates for shape C are (___, ___), (___, ___), (___, ___).

d Complete the sentence below.

Shape ___ has been translated 6 units to make shape ___ .

Exercise 15E Compass directions and turns

This exercise will give you practice in

○ understanding compass point directions

Jenny made this map of the places she visited in London.

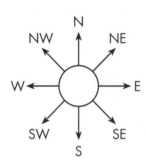

Madame Tussauds

London Zoo

Alexandra Palace

Heathrow

Buckingham Palace

St Paul's Cathedral

Westminster Abbey

Millennium Eye

Canary Wharf

1 Which building or place is:

a west of the Millennium Eye? _____

b north of Buckingham Palace? _____

c south of St Paul's Cathedral? _____

2 You are at Buckingham Palace, which building or place is:

a to the north-east? _____

b to the south-west? _____

3 You are still at Buckingham Palace. Face Heathrow Airport. Turn clockwise through 90°. Which direction are you facing? What can you see?

_____

4 You are on the Millennium Eye. Face Buckingham Palace. Turn to face the north-east. What can you see?

_____

Exercise 16A From bar-line charts to line graphs (continuous data)

This exercise will give you practice in

- drawing a temperature–time bar-line graph and using it to solve problems

During his summer holidays, Jack recorded the temperatures in his garden on 22nd August. The results are shown in the table on the right.

Time	Temperature (°C)
7.30 am	12
8.30 am	14
9.30 am	16
10.30 am	16
11.30 am	20
12.30 pm	22

1 What was the temperature at 9.30 am? _____

2 When was the temperature 20°C? _____

3 Draw a bar-line chart for the data on the axes below.

4 Join up the tops of the bars on your graph using a ruler.

5 What was the temperature at 11.00 am?

_____

6 Between what times was the temperature the same?

_____

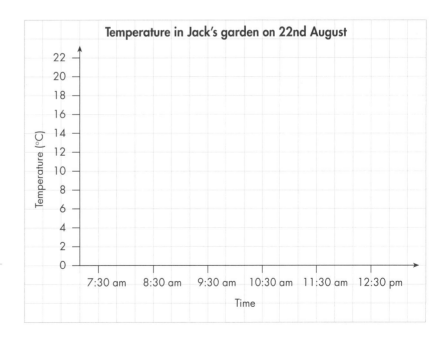

Exercise 16B Line graphs (continuous data)

This exercise will give you practice in

- reading data represented in a temperature–time line graph

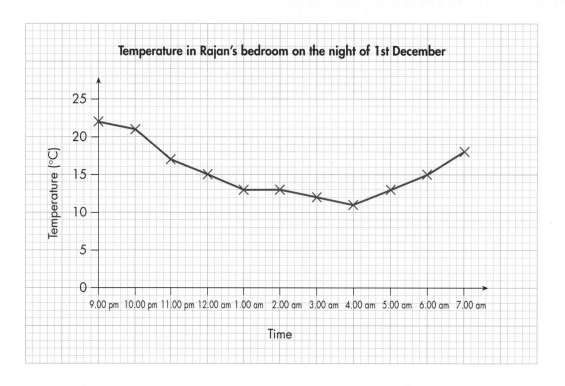

The graph shows the temperature in Rajan's bedroom one night.

1 What was the temperature at 11.00 pm? _____

2 When was the temperature 21°C? _____

3 When was it hottest? _____

4 What was the coldest temperature? _____

5 Between what times did the temperature stay the same? _____

6 After what time did the temperature start to rise? _____

Complete the table by reading the data from the graph.

Time	Temperature (°C)
9.00 pm	22
10.00 pm	21
11.00 pm	17
12.00 am	15
1.00 am	13
2.00 am	13
3.00 am	
4.00 am	
5.00 am	
6.00 am	
7.00 am	

Exercise 16C Distance–time line graphs

This exercise will give you practice in

- solving problems by reading a distance–time line graph

Alice delivers post in her van. The line graph shows her journey.

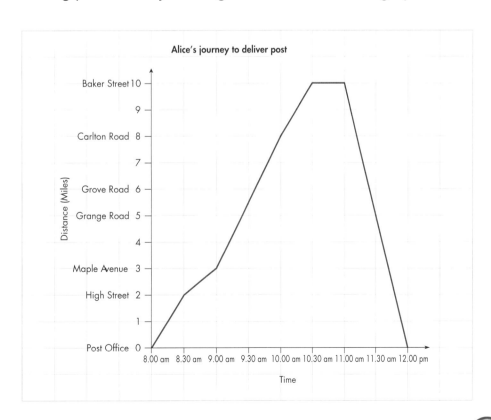

1 Where did Alice deliver post first? What time did she get there?

2 Where was her next stop? How far is it from the post office?

3 What do you think was happening between 10:30 and 11:00?

4 What time did Alice start her return journey to the post office? _____

5 How far is Carlton Road from the post office? _____

6 What time did Alice get back to the post office? _____

Exercise 16D   Line graphs (discrete data)

This exercise will give you practice in

- solving problems by drawing and reading data from a line graph

Surround Sounds are having a CD sale. The owner has placed this poster in the window of the shop.

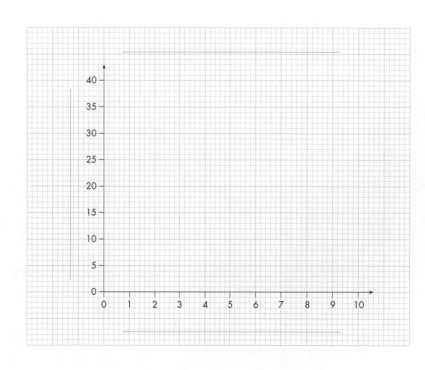

Surround Sounds
MASSIVE
CD Sale!

Number of CDs Bought	Price
1	£5
2	£9
3	£13
4	£17
5	£21
6	£25
7	£29
8	£33
9	£36
10	£36

1) Label the axes on the graph and give the graph a title.

2) How much do 0 CDs cost? _____ Plot this point on the graph.

3) How much does one CD cost? _____ Plot this point on the graph.

4) Continue plotting the points on the graph.

5) Join up your points.

6) How much do eight CDs cost? _____

7) Do you think that buying two CDs instead of one CD is value for money?
Explain your answer.

_____

_____

8) Why do you think that the price for nine CDs is the same as for 10 CDs?

_____

_____

Exercise 17A Adding decimals

This exercise will give you practice in
- adding pairs of decimals

1 Work out the answers to each of these.

    a £16.43 + £12.56   **b** £12.67 + £11.99   **c** £14.56 + £19.60

    d £22.64 + £26.89   **e** £24.99 + £29.99   **f** £34.56 + £44.21

2 Calculate each of the following.

    a 4.51 m + 3.85 m   **b** 5.65 m + 4.78 m   **c** 9.7 m + 6.2 m

    d 9.65 m + 3.92 m   **e** 12.3 m + 13.6 m   **f** 18.65 m + 14.72 m

Work out the answers to each of these.

a   9.65 kg + 3.67 kg

b   10.73 kg + 11.98 kg

c   21.33 kg + 66.73 kg

d   78.45 kg + 82.34 kg

e   79.65 kg + 89.54 kg

f   88.56 kg + 44.76 kg

Exercise 17B Subtracting decimals

This exercise will give you practice in
- subtracting pairs of decimals

Work out the answers to each of these.

a   £46.12 – £37.08

b   £37.43 – £28.27

c   £56.43 – £31.85

d   £86.42 – £36.56

e   £88.42 – £63.45

f   £93.45 – £52.56

2 Calculate each of the following.

    a   8.63 m – 4.35 m   **b**   14.3 cm – 9.6 cm   **c**   17.83 m – 14.62 m

    d   18.6 km – 15.9 km   **e**   24.45 m – 19.34 m   **f**   34.62 km – 23.95 km

3 Work out the answers to each of the following.

    a   23.4 kg – 12.6 kg   **b**   19.58 kg – 11.01 kg   **c**   33.25 kg – 29.88 kg

    d   78.21 kg – 70.56 kg   **e**   90.84 kg – 87.65 kg   **f**   33.3 kg – 29.9 kg

Exercise 17C **Multiplying decimals**

This exercise will give you practice in

- estimating
- multiplying decimals

Partition each of these numbers into whole numbers and decimal numbers.
The first one has been done for you.

a 4.3 $= 4.0 + 0.3$ **b** 2.4 _____   **c** 5.6 _____

d 6.5 _____   **e** 7.5 _____   **f** 7.7 _____

g 8.2 _____   **h** 1.8 _____   **i** 9.5 _____

j 2.9 _____   **k** 3.6 _____   **l** 9.9 _____

Work out the answer to each of these decimal multiplications following the
steps below.

   1 write down an estimate

   2 work out the calculation by partitioning the whole numbers from the decimal numbers

The first one has been done for you.

a 4.3×4

   Estimate: $4 \times 4 = 16$

            $4.0 \times 4 = 16$

            $0.3 \times 4 = 1.2$

                 $= 17.2$

b 7.8×4

c 6.5×4

d 4.6×5

e 5.6×4

f 9.9×5

g 5.8 × 4

_____

_____

_____

_____

h 6.2 × 5

_____

_____

_____

_____

i 6.3 × 4

_____

_____

_____

_____

j 4.9 × 6

_____

_____

_____

_____

Exercise 17D Problem solving

This exercise will give you practice in

- using addition, subtraction, multiplication and division to solve real-life problems

Work out each of the following problems. Explain briefly the method you used to solve the problem.

1 On Saturday I spent £24.50 on clothes. I bought a t-shirt costing £7.80 and a cap for £ 5.65. I spent the rest of the money on a jumper. How much did the jumper cost?

_____

_____

_____

_____

2 968 students from Years 7, 8 and 9 went on a trip to a museum. If there are 334 students in Year 7 and 318 in Year 8, how many students are in Year 9?

_____

_____

_____

_____

3 The ICT department spent £1065 on new equipment. £709 was spent on new printers and £223 on keyboards. The rest of the money was used to buy a digital camera. How much did the camera cost?

4 Year 7 raised £235.89 for a local charity. The sponsored walk raised £145.50 and the cake sale raised £56.32. The rest of the money was raised through a non-uniform day. How much was raised for the non-uniform day?

Exercise 17E Capacity

This exercise will give you practice in
- using and writing measures of capacity such as *l* and *ml*.

1 Draw a line between the two capacities that are the same. Circle the odd one out.

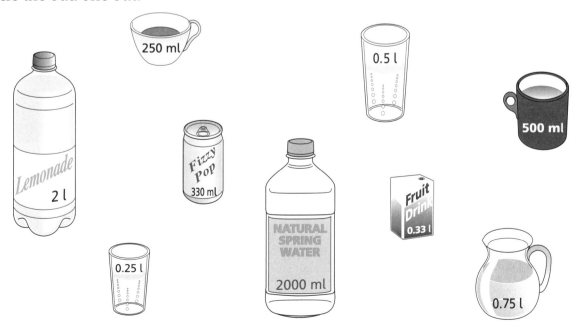

2 A Year 7 class were going on a school trip. They bought the following drinks.

a Change the capacity from millilitres into litres. Record your answers in decimal form i
the space provided.

b What is the capacity of two cans of coke and two cartons of orange juice? Record your
answer in millilitres and litres. _____

_____

c What is the capacity of three cartons of apple juice and two cartons of fruit drink?
Write your answer in millilitres and litres. _____

_____

d What is the capacity of all the drinks in total? Write your answer in millilitres
and litres. _____

_____

Exercise 17F **Weight**

This exercise will give you practice in
- using and writing units of mass such as kg and g

1 Write these weights in grams. The first one has been done for you.

a $5\frac{1}{2}$ kg   *= 5000 g + 500 g = 5500 g* _____

b $3\frac{1}{4}$ kg   _____

c $6\frac{3}{4}$ kg _____

d $4\frac{1}{10}$ kg _____

Write these weights in kilograms and grams. The first one has been done for you.

a 6500 g = *6000 g + 500 g = 6 kg 500 g* _____

b 3256 g _____

c 7560 g _____

d 4700 g _____

e 6640 g _____

Choose three standard weights to balance each of the following totals. The first one has been done for you.

a 530 g   = *500 g + 20 g + 10 g* _____

b 720 g _____

c 270 g _____

d 570 g _____

e 80 g _____

Choose four standard weights to balance these totals.

a 1800 g _____

b 330 g _____

c 1350 g _____

d 1080 g _____

Exercise 18A **Polygons**

This exercise will give you practice in

- classifying 2-D shapes according to regularity, symmetry and angles

1 Look at the shapes below. Decide whether each shape is regular or irregular and write the letter of each shape in the correct box.

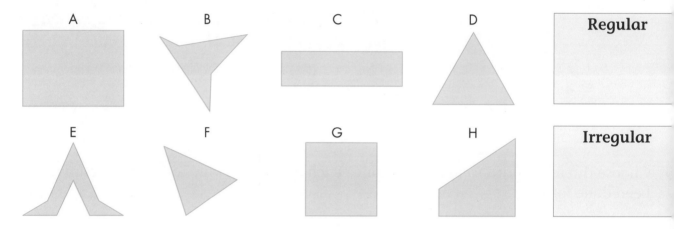

	Regular

	Irregular

2 Look at the shapes below. Decide whether each contains at least 1 right angle or not. Write the letter of each shape in the correct box.

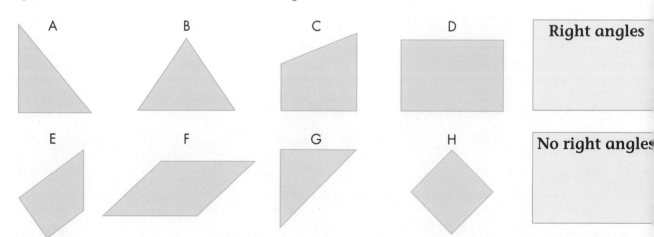

	Right angles

	No right angles

Look at the shapes below. Decide whether each has either no lines of symmetry or one or more lines of symmetry. Write the letter of each shape in the correct box.

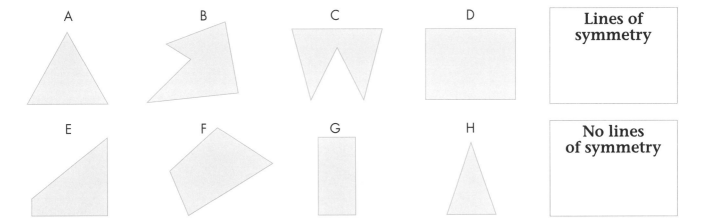

Exercise 18B Tessellations

This exercise will give you practice in

○ recognising and extending patterns of shapes

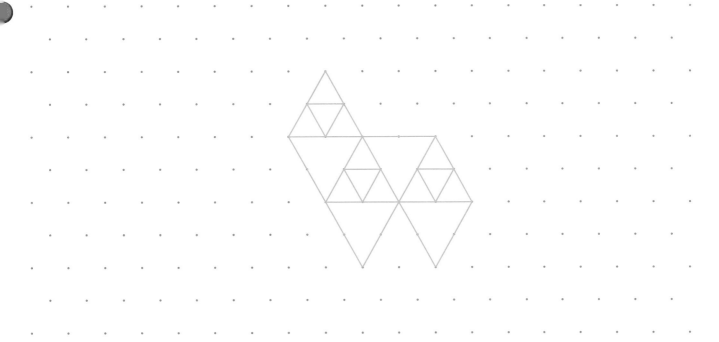

a Continue the pattern until you cannot fit any more triangles on the page.

b Colour your pattern so that triangles next to each other do not have the same colour. Use the least number of colours possible.

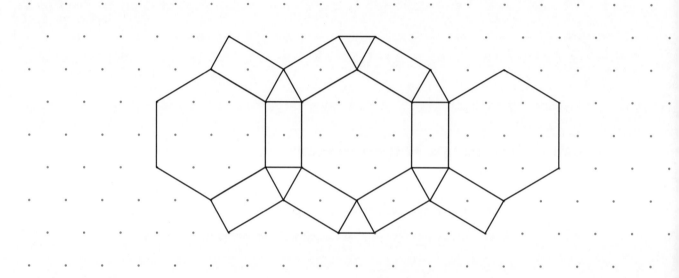

a   Name all of the shapes used to make this pattern. _____

_____

b   Continue the pattern until you cannot fit any more shapes on the page.

c   Colour your pattern so that shapes next to each other do not have the same
colour. Use the least number of colours possible.

Exercise 18C 3-D shapes

This exercise will give you practice in
- classifying 3-D shapes

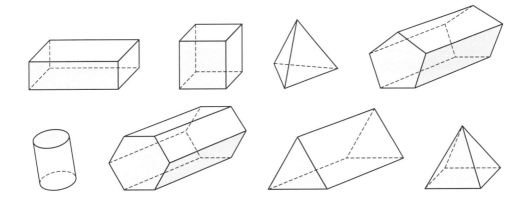

Complete the table below by classifying the 3-D shapes above.

Shape	Number of faces	Number of vertices	Is it a polyhedron	Is it a prism?
Cube	6	8	Yes	Yes

a Which shape is not a prism or a polyhedron? _____

b Why is this? _____

_____

Which of the 3-D shapes have at least one square face? _____

4 Which of the 3-D shapes have at least one triangular face? _____

_____

5 Which shape appears in the answer to both **Questions 3** and **4**?

_____

6 **a** Which shapes have all identical faces? _____

b What type of shapes are these faces? _____

Published by Collins
An imprint of HarperCollins*Publishers*
77–85 Fulham Palace Road
Hammersmith
London
W6 8JB

Browse the complete Collins catalogue at
www.collinseducation.com

Helen and Simon Greaves assert their moral rights to be identified
as the authors of this work.

Original edition by Jaqueline Kaye.

British Library Cataloguing in Publication Data
A Catalogue record for this publication is available from the
British Library

Commissioned by Katie Sergeant
Design and typesetting by Newgen
Edited by Karen Westall
Project managed by Sue Chapple
Proofread by Margaret Shepherd
Illustrations by Nigel Jordan and Tony Wilkins
Covers by Oculus Design and Communications
Production by Simon Moore
Printed and bound by Printing Express, Hong Kong

NEW MATHS FRAMEWORKING

Helen and Simon Greaves

Year 7, Workbook

Collins New Maths Frameworking matches the new KS3 Framework for Teaching Mathematics and the new Programme of Study providing full support for teachers and the right progression for all levels.

This workbook provides extra support and practice to help students make a smooth transition from Key Stage 2 to Key Stage 3.

Questions match topics covered in Year 7 Pupil Book 1 to ensure easy progression

Full colour, write-in layout makes activities accessible and personal

Pupil-friendly learning objectives set clear targets and aid self-assessment

Hundreds of questions provide excellent practice at the right level

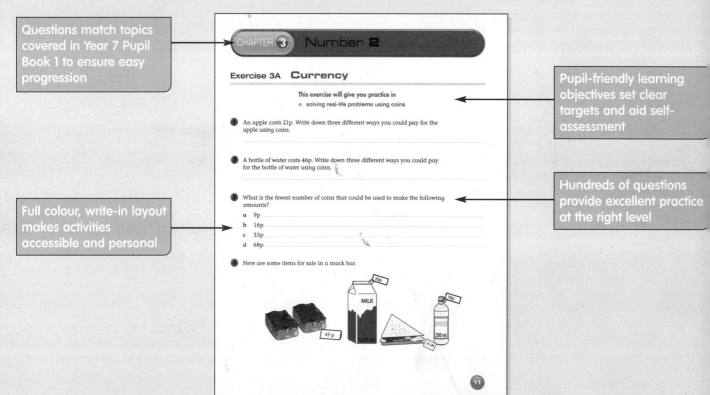

Year 7 Additional Support Teacher's Pack 978-0-00-726794-1

Network licence also available 978-0-00-726795-8

Find out more at: www.collinseducation.com/newmathsframeworking

Browse the complete Collins catalogu

www.collinseducation.cc

ISBN 978-0-00-726790-3

9 780007 267903

FSC